HAL•LEONARD INSTRUMENTAL PLAY-ALONG

AUDIO ACCESS INCLUDED

PLAYBACK+
Speed • Pitch • Balance • Loop

VIOLIN

Gospel Hymns

T0066491

To access audio visit:
www.halleonard.com/mylibrary

Enter Code
2606-5406-7604-5517

ISBN 978-1-4950-7386-1

HAL•LEONARD®

7777 W. BLUEMOUND RD. P.O. BOX 13819 MILWAUKEE, WI 53213

In Australia Contact:
Hal Leonard Australia Pty. Ltd.
4 Lentara Court
Cheltenham, Victoria, 3192 Australia
Email: ausadmin@halleonard.com.au

Visit Hal Leonard Online at
www.halleonard.com

AMAZING GRACE

VIOLIN

Words by JOHN NEWTON
Traditional American Melody

BLESSED ASSURANCE

VIOLIN

Lyrics by FANNY J. CROSBY
Music by PHOEBE PALMER KNAPP

DOWN BY THE RIVERSIDE

VIOLIN

African American Spiritual

HE'S GOT THE WHOLE WORLD IN HIS HANDS

VIOLIN

Traditional Spiritual

HIS EYE IS ON THE SPARROW

VIOLIN

Words by CIVILLA D. MARTIN
Music by CHARLES H. GABRIEL

IN THE GARDEN

VIOLIN

Words and Music by
C. AUSTIN MILES

LEANING ON THE EVERLASTING ARMS

VIOLIN

Words by ELISHA A. HOFFMAN
Music by ANTHONY J. SHOWALTER

THE OLD RUGGED CROSS

VIOLIN

Words and Music by
REV. GEORGE BENNARD

PRECIOUS MEMORIES

VIOLIN

Words and Music by
J.B.F. WRIGHT

SHALL WE GATHER AT THE RIVER?

VIOLIN

Words and Music by
ROBERT LOWRY

SWEET BY AND BY

VIOLIN

Words by SANFORD FILLMORE BENNETT
Music by JOSEPH P. WEBSTER

THERE IS POWER IN THE BLOOD

VIOLIN

Words and Music by
LEWIS E. JONES

Quickly, with energy
Lap steel guitar

Play

mf

f

1.

2.

WAYFARING STRANGER

VIOLIN

Southern American Folk Hymn

WHEN WE ALL GET TO HEAVEN

VIOLIN

Words by ELIZA E. HEWITT
Music by EMILY D. WILSON

WHISPERING HOPE

VIOLIN

Words and Music by
ALICE HAWTHORNE